Spooky America

THE

GHOSTLY TALES

OF

NEWPORT

JENNIFER CAMERON

Adapted from *Ghosts of Newport* by John T. Brennan

arcadia®
CHILDREN'S BOOKS

MASSACHUSETTS

RHODE
ISLAND

CONNECTICUT

ATLANTIC OCEAN

NEWPORT

Table of Contents & Map Key

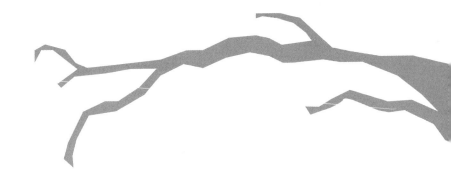

Introduction

Rhode Islanders have always been free thinkers—they are rebels and revolutionaries. When you come from the smallest state in America you need big, bold ideas to set yourself apart. And the people from Newport, Rhode Island, have always had big and bold ideas. With all that energy running through their veins, is it really surprising so many Newporters don't rest quietly in death?

History gives the Pilgrims, who landed in Plymouth, Massachusetts, in 1620, a lot of credit for the founding of America. They came to the New World seeking religious freedom. But too bad for any person who wanted religious freedom from the Pilgrims! If you wanted to live outside the rules of the Pilgrims, well, then you were exiled, which meant you were kicked out of the community. And if you refused to be exiled, you were executed.

Anne Hutchinson was one of those people who chose exile. She, and others like her, left Massachusetts in 1638 and went south to live peacefully with the native Narragansett tribe on what they called Aquidneck Island. Within a year, two of Anne's followers, William Coddington and Nicholas Easton, moved a bit farther south and founded Newport in 1639. Their belief in a person's right to the freedom of thought and religion was so strong that they made these freedoms part of Newport's laws in 1641. Coddington and the other Newporters believed in the separation of church and state, meaning government couldn't interfere in religion.

This was a pretty radical idea at the time, but the founders were committed to seeing how it would work. When they received their royal charter to form a colony in 1663, they promised to "hold forth a lively experiment . . . to form a government as the people may choose . . . with a full liberty in religious commitments."

And with that, Newporters created a government for and by the people. They promised you could worship if and as you pleased. Such freedoms became a blueprint for the foundation of our nation.

It was part of the reason behind Rhode Island's motto: First in war; Last in peace. Rhode Islanders had never cared much for the heavy restrictions placed on them by the British government, so they declared independence from England a full two months before the rest of the colonies. First in war!

After the Revolutionary War, Rhode Islanders weren't too thrilled with early drafts of the Constitution. They demanded it include language guaranteeing the freedom of religion and refused to sign on until it did. Last in peace!

Rhode Islanders have never been afraid to speak their minds and make their voices heard in life. Is it any wonder they expect to be heard in death as well?

Dying to Get In

When you come to Newport via the Newport Bridge, you will find yourself on Farewell Street. It is aptly named, but not because you've bid goodbye to the mainland. Farewell Street is lined by numerous cemeteries. So many bodies are buried here that Farewell Street has more dead people per mile than any other street in America!

How did these cemeteries get so full? In colonial times, cemeteries were not that common. People were buried in family plots on family land or they were buried in churchyards. But what if there was no family land? What if the churchyard was full? What if there was so much building and growth that empty space was hard to find?

In 1640, Dr. John Clarke donated some of his land to be used as a graveyard for commoners and travelers in Newport. You didn't have to belong to a certain church or have money in order to be buried here. The land became known as the Common Burying Ground, and it has more colonial headstones than any other American cemetery.

If you choose to visit, it's best to go in the bright light of day. It's not because ghosts come out at night. (They usually do.) It's because so many of these old headstones are really hard to read. In the dark, they look like nothing more than blank pieces of slate.

There is something else that makes the Common Burying Ground uniquely special. It isn't just the high number of graves in a small space or the fact that famous citizens (for their time) are buried here among everyday Newporters. It's not even the wide variety of races and religions who share this "resting" place together. It is the fascinating carvings found on a number of the headstones and the story of the man who put them there.

In the northernmost part of the Common Burying Ground is a section named God's Little Acre. Here, you will find the gravestones of free Africans, indentured servants, and enslaved people.

Think the northern colonies didn't have slaves? Think again. The *Sea Flower* was the first ship to bring enslaved people to

Newport . . . and that ship docked in the harbor in 1696. Slaves were put to work as maids and servants, sailors and wharfmen. Even more were given apprenticeships and taught a trade. Colonial Newport needed all the skilled workers it could get.

One man who desperately needed skilled workers was John Stevens. In the early 1700s, John was the only stonecutter in Newport, and he wasn't very good at his work. His carvings were shallow and sloppy and have barely survived the passage of time.

Although he wasn't very good at his craft, he made sure his son and his grandson became skilled, and both men were quite renowned for their work. As was Zingo Stevens, John's slave. (Like many Newport slaves, Zingo took his master's last name but was allowed to keep his African name as his first name.)

Zingo Stevens was a very good stonecutter, and his work is seen throughout the Common Burying

Ground, particularly in God's Little Acre. When Zingo finished work for his owner, he was allowed to work for his own wages and was frequently commissioned to carve headstones for free Africans as well as enslaved people. Although he carved the typical designs of the time— skulls, hourglasses, and panel decorations—his cherubs and angels were different. He carved them with African features.

It was also common at the time to carve a likeness of the person who died on their headstone. When Zingo carved stones for other Africans, he depicted them in the traditional African dress of their culture. And he signed the stones, making them the oldest confirmed African American art in our country.

It is said spirits will haunt spaces where they have unfinished business. From the money Zingo earned doing his own work, he managed to buy his freedom. He also helped found the

Free African Union Society, a benevolence group for free Africans that offered a form of health care and life insurance and looked after widows and orphans. Records show he left Newport, but there is no record that says where he went.

There is no ghostly record either.

Zingo's business in Newport, in his community, in the Common Burying Ground, and in God's Little Acre was definitely finished. It is work well done. Rest in peace, Zingo Stevens. Wherever you are.

There are Newport spirits though who have not rested. One ghost in the Common Burying Ground definitely wants to make himself known. Visitors who have seen him say he wanders about the graveyard as if lost. Locals believe his headstone was one of those destroyed when British troops used the graveyard for target practice during the Revolutionary War. Maybe his headstone was stolen—having a headstone at all was quite the luxury. Maybe it's so old, the ghost can no longer read it?

Whatever the reason, the lost ghost is just one of many souls seen roaming Newport's cemeteries. Another spirit seems be on the lookout for vandals and folks who are up to no good. People visiting swear they feel like they are being carefully watched and that the watcher is not friendly. In another cemetery, a Narragansett woman is seen floating above her grave with crossed arms and a stern expression. Is she waiting for something? Or someone? If so, she's been waiting for over 300 years.

So, how do we know spirits have been wandering the Farewell Street cemeteries for so long? Because the first reported sighting of ghosts and eerie lights hovering over graves in the Common Burying Ground was recorded in 1702!

CHAPTER 2

Pirates and Plunder and Nazis!

As you step past the gravestones in the Common Burying Ground, you can't really tell how many people are entombed beneath the earth in Newport. Some stones have been destroyed. Some have been stolen. For some, there was never a stone to begin with.

They were poor. They were victims of plague. Or they were purposefully denied a quiet resting place because of their crimes.

And what kind of misdeeds could cause such punishment? Read on.

In Colonial times, Newporters earned money as slavers and whalers. They earned money as shipbuilders. They earned money making and selling some of the world's best rum, candles, and chocolate.

But some Newporters earned a whole lot of money as pirates!

The British government called these people privateers. Privateers were given legal licenses by the British government to hunt, harass, and loot "enemy" vessels. Who was the enemy? The French, Spanish, and Dutch. If you sailed ships under those flags, you better watch the horizon!

Sometimes those enemy ships were hard to find. Sometimes it was much easier to "mistakenly" loot and destroy a British ship. And sometimes you got caught.

Newport did its best to keep antipiracy laws very relaxed. If you weren't caught in the act of piracy you couldn't be accused of it or brought to trial for it. With laws such as that, Newport became a haven for the licensed and the lawless—the privateer and the pirate.

GHOSTS OF GRAVELLY POINT

By 1716, the British government was rethinking its privateer plan. It seems privateers kept "mistaking" British ships for enemy ships. In other words, the privateers kept sinking and stealing from the wrong side! The British Admiralty pushed Rhode Island's government to get a grip on the pirate problem. It was time to bring the lawless to justice. But who would have guessed it would be so ghastly?

In the spring of 1723, the notorious and cruel Edward Low captained the pirate ship *Fortune*. His sidekick, Charles Harris, sailed beside him on the *Ranger*. Together, they hunted the ocean looking for ships to plunder and burn.

As they sailed off the New York coast, the *Fortune* and *Ranger* spotted what they thought was a whaling ship. It was actually the *Greyhound*—a British warship with twenty cannons and orders to arrest all pirates.

Captain Low managed to break away and flee. Captain Harris was not so lucky. The *Greyhound* easily caught him and thirty-four other crew members of the *Ranger*.

The pirates were brought to Newport to face trial. A few were shown mercy, but twenty-six men were found guilty of piracy.

All twenty-six would be executed by hanging at Gravelly Point on July 19, 1723. But that was not the end of their punishment.

Their bodies were covered in tar, so they would take longer to rot, and they were left to hang at Gravelly Point through the long, hot summer as a warning to other pirates. It sent a clear message: Newport was no longer a safe haven for their kind.

When the bodies were finally cut down in October, they were taken to Newport's Goat Island—a small bit of land in the Narragansett Bay—and thrown into an unmarked grave. It was unmarked because the spot where they were buried is at a point between low and high tide. This truly was a final punishment—the constant ebb and flow of the waves would make sure their souls could find no rest. The hanging of the *Ranger's* crew remains the largest public execution in our country's history.

Today, if you take the bridge over to Goat Island and sit on the seawall, you can watch the sailboats dance across Narragansett Bay and listen to the gulls as they circle the incoming fishing boats. Or maybe instead you'll see ghostly lights bobbing under the water and hear the agonized cries of twenty-six pirates. Locals and visitors alike report seeing and hearing just that.

THE PALATINE LIGHT

Pirates don't always come after you on the ocean. Sometimes they wait until you get to shore.

About twelve miles off the coast of Newport sits a small, somewhat porkchop-shaped bit of land called Block Island. It is made up of bluffs, beaches, and the Great Salt Pond. If you like to surf, swim, or build sandcastles, the seventeen miles of Block Island coastline are the perfect place to spend a summer day.

But in the 1730s, the Block Island coastline was a terrible place to spend a winter's night! A tragedy that happened there left a confusing tale of cruelty and murder, courage and sacrifice, and it also left Rhode Island with its most enduring and well-documented ghost story—the Palatine Light!

In 1738, the British ship *Princess Augusta* picked up about 240 emigrants from a region in southern Germany known as the Palatinate. Since the emigrants were called Palatines, their ship became known as the *Palatine*. Captain George Long, his inexperienced crew, and their passengers set sail for Philadelphia in August.

The *Palatine* was a "bad luck" ship from the start. Water supplied for the voyage was contaminated, and soon, half the crew, including Captain Long, and more than half the passengers were dead. The *Palatine* was beset with bad weather and winds that continually pushed it off course. The six-week voyage turned into a sixteen-week ordeal with freezing winter temperatures and vanishing food supplies.

Andrew Brook, the former first mate who now led as captain, tried in vain to land the leaking and creaking ship in New York or Newport instead of Philadelphia, since the winter gales kept pushing them north.

On December 27, during a true New England nor'easter (a winter storm made up of snow, sleet, and wind), the crew spotted what they thought was the Montauk Light coming from the lighthouse on Long Island. They headed for it, but the ship ran aground on the shoals surrounding Block Island.

With the *Palatine* now wrecked and pounded by surf as well as the storm, Captain Brook and his crew abandoned ship and rowed to shore— without their passengers! That's right. They left the remaining Palatines to suffer their fate throughout the long December night.

Now the story splits into several versions. Block Islanders say the crew begged and pleaded with Captain Brook until he finally allowed them to brave the sea and rescue all passengers that remained alive.

According to the crew, Captain Brook bravely faced the storm and rowed to shore to get help. He left the passengers on ship to keep them sheltered and safe. He brought the crew with him in case there was trouble. Block Island had a reputation for harboring "wreckers." (Wreckers were people who robbed victims and looted ships that wrecked on the beach.)

Once Brook felt sure the passengers would be safe, he and his crew rowed back through the waves and rescued all the passengers as well as their belongings. Even after the ship broke up, Brook ordered the crew continue to retrieve cargo until they found all they could.

But there is another account that tells a darker story. In this version, the *Palatine* was lured to the rocks by a false light. Lighthouses were critical in guiding ships to safe harbors and warning them about hidden reefs and dangerous shores. So to light a false lamp and purposefully direct a ship to its doom was a horrible thing to do.

Block Islanders lived a sparse and challenging life while the bustle and wealth of Newport lay just miles across the water. It is documented that Block Islanders were accused of lighting false lights so they could loot the wrecked ships. Ships' captains would go out of their way to avoid the island and those who lived there.

Was it a false light the crew of the *Palatine* saw? Or had months of illness and hunger, bad weather, and bad water caused them to see a beacon that was not there? Regardless, these later accounts also say that while the *Palatine* lay crippled, wreckers from the island descended on it. They looted and plundered the cargo and murdered any survivors who would not join them.

Even though there are various accounts of that evening, there are a few things they all agree on. The *Palatine* was too damaged to repair. To leave it on the rocks was too hazardous to other ships. When the storm subsided, the *Palatine* was towed into deeper water, set on fire, and sunk.

It is also agreed that there was a woman still on the ship who was either forgotten or who refused to leave and abandon her property. As the ship burned, she burned with it, and her screams echoed across the water.

Soon after this tragedy, on dark December nights between Christmas and New Year's Eve, islanders and sailors alike began seeing the ghostly form of a burning ship sail off the coast of Block Island—and with it, they heard the terrified screams of a woman who suffered a horrible fate.

It is said to see the *Palatine* Light is a bad omen. Disaster awaits those who witness it, and tragic storms will soon arrive to wreak havoc. Legend says the *Palatine* Light will continue to burn and haunt Block Island until the pirates, or their descendants, atone for their evil deeds.

Sightings have been recorded since then, including one in 1969. In that sighting, a crowd of people witnessed "a large, glowing fireball" off the coast of the island, near Sandy Point. An investigation revealed no known source for the spectral glow. But believers in the *Palatine* Light know the source.

If you like swimming or shell collecting, hit the sandy beaches of Block Island in the summer. But if you want ghosts, screams in the night, and the phantom shape of a blazing ship on the horizon, take the ferry to Block Island in late December . . . if you dare!

LAST MINUTES OF THE MINERVA

The Block Island coastline isn't the only one that hides danger under the waves. And it isn't the only one haunted by a ghostly ship.

On the southwestern tip of Newport, where the Narragansett Bay meets the Atlantic Ocean, you will find Brenton Point and Brenton Point State Park. Tucked deep in the woods of the park are the ruins of a Gilded Age mansion named The Reef—a place that has a ghost story all its own. (You'll read more about that later!) A real reef—Brenton Reef—lies just off the coast and is the reason for the spectacular surf that crashes onto Brenton Point. The reef's jagged rocks and powerful currents are also the reason for numerous shipwrecks and drownings. Over the centuries, so many bodies have been pulled from these waters that the area is commonly called Graves Point.

Whether the crew of the Spanish ship *Minerva* knew this or not, they were about to find out just how dangerous Brenton Point could be.

It was another December night—Christmas Eve—in 1810, when the *Minerva* found itself in a ferocious nor'easter with hurricane-force winds and blizzard-like snow. It was a merchant ship loaded with rum and wine, gold, silver, and coins. It also carried a minute gun, which was used to send distress signals, with one fired every minute.

On that bleak December night, the *Minerva* just needed to get past Brenton Point to reach Newport's safe harbor. It wouldn't make it. The storm threw it onto the reef and pounded it into the rocks. The desperate crew began firing the minute gun as the storm, waves, and reef tore the ship to pieces.

The storm was so intense rescue boats could not be launched. People on the mainland could only stand in the sleet and snow and listen to the cries of the sailors, the grinding of the ship's hull, and the booming gun firing its plea for help. Ten sailors died that night, and the *Minerva* was broken in pieces and strewn across the reef. Miraculously, nine men were pulled alive from the wild waters.

If you visit Brenton Point you will probably be struck by its scenic beauty and spectacular views. If you visit on a calm day, you will hear the cries of the ever-present gulls hovering over the sea. You will not be aware of the turmoil and danger that hides just beneath the waves. But if you go on a day of wild weather, especially in December, especially at night, you will surely hear the crashing of the surf and the rumble of the ocean.

Listen closely, and you may also hear the terrified cries of sailors struggling to keep their ship and themselves alive. You may hear the thundering groans of a ship being torn to pieces. And you may surely hear the bang of a minute gun counting down the time until all is lost. Locals swear you will hear these things.

They swear the *Minerva* still haunts the waters, seeking a safe harbor it will never find. The area isn't known as Graves Point for nothing.

HUNTING A MODERN MOBY DICK

There are many ships, or bits of ships, that lay scattered across the bottom of the Narragansett Bay and along the shores of Rhode Island. Storm-tossed seas, unseen rocks, and reefs are the cause of their demise. But there is one ship—or boat rather—that was put on the bottom quite deliberately.

In 1944, the United States had been at war with Germany and the other Axis powers for three long years. Although most of the battles were waged in far-off places in Europe and Asia, there were smaller battles taking place across the Atlantic Ocean, up and down the East Coast, and around Newport, where the Naval War College is located.

The German U-boat *U-853* (similar to a submarine) was threatening merchant and troop supply ships. It was spotted preparing to attack the HMS *Queen Mary*, which was carrying hundreds of American troops to Europe and to war, so the escort carrier USS *Croatan* and six destroyers were sent to hunt the U-boat down.

U-853's captain was so skilled that for three weeks, he managed to evade his hunters, fend off attacks, and submerge and hide. In fact, *U-853* proved so hard to find that the *Croatan's* crew nicknamed it "Moby Dick," after the elusive white whale in Herman Melville's novel of the same name.

In April 1945, Moby Dick sank the USS *Eagle* off the coast of Maine. It then made its way down to hide in the currents around Newport and wait for another victim. On May 5, the leaders in Germany ordered all U-boats to stop attacking the enemy and return home—World War II was almost over. Moby Dick did not get the message. Or maybe the captain ignored it. Either way, on that same day, it torpedoed the stern off the SS *Black Point*. The *Black Point* sank in fifteen minutes, taking twelve of its crew members with it. As the SS *Kamen* rescued the remaining thirty-four sailors, the *Kamen's* captain radioed the Navy—there was a U-boat in the area!

A "hunter-killer" group was formed with four American warships and at least two blimps. Moby Dick tried running. It tried hiding. It would not escape. For sixteen hours, the hunter-killer group bombed and depth-charged the area. Finally, on May 6, debris, oil, charts, and an officer's cap floated to the surface of the sea. Moby Dick—*U-853* was the last submarine sunk in American waters during World War II.

Moby Dick sits a few miles off the coast of Newport with its crew entombed within it. It lies in 113 feet of water, which is deep but not so deep that experienced divers can't reach it. In 1960, a diver entered the wreck and came back to the surface with the bones of one of the crew! (The bones were buried with full military honors in Newport's Island Cemetery Annex.)

The disturbance of the wreck and the removal of the sailor's remains caused the US government to declare *U-853* a gravesite, and divers are now forbidden to enter the submarine and disturb those who rest there.

But that doesn't keep the ones who rest there from disturbing divers. People who dive on the wreck have mentioned strange noises

coming from the sunken U-boat—noises they can clearly hear 113 feet under the sea. Other divers swear they feel the presence of spirits around them, phantoms lurking in the shadowy depths. Are these ghosts of the German crew looking for their missing shipmate? Or are they just protecting their remains from anymore meddling? Whatever their reason, they are a good reminder that not every ghost haunts on dry land.

Rose Island Lighthouse

A Rose by Any Other Name . . . Would Still Be Haunted

If you know Newport, it comes as no surprise that enemy ships and submarines used to troll the area. The US Navy has been the major employer in and around Newport for over a century.

Founded in 1883, Naval Station Newport is home to the Naval War College, the

Naval Justice School, and the Navy's Officer Candidate School. It is the location of the Naval Undersea Warfare Center and conducts "testing and evaluation of advanced undersea warfare systems" (which probably translates into doing cool secret stuff underwater).

Newport and its famous harbor have been historically important to the US military—particularly the US Navy—from the Revolutionary War to the present day. During World War II, over 80 percent of all the Navy's torpedoes were built in Newport and stored on nearby Rose Island. That's where we'll find our next ghosts.

A mere mile from Naval Station Newport, out in Narragansett Bay, Rose Island is in a good location to support the naval station and defend the harbor. In 1798, the United States took over the island and began building Fort Hamilton. (Yes, named for *that* Hamilton— Alexander.) Work was never completed on the fort, but enough work was done to make it usable for troop training and for quarantining the sick. The fort's walls are over three feet thick, and so during wartime, it became the perfect place to store hundreds of thousands of pounds of explosives. If something went boom

in the night, it should stay contained in the fort. But the ghosts that went bump in the night couldn't be contained within the abandoned and crumbling ruins.

During the 1700s and 1800s, Newport was a major center of trade . . . and infectious disease. With so many people coming and going from all over the world, the city fell victim to epidemics like smallpox, typhoid, and tuberculosis. To keep Newporters safe, Rose Island became the city's sick ward. Many ill and suffering people were sent to Rose Island. Not so many would leave.

Today, it is reported that lights glow and flash within the fort, although it's not wired with electricity. Doors open and close while no one is there. Faint, muttering voices are heard coming from the quarantine rooms. Are those quiet voices people whispering their final goodbyes? Are the lights those carried by healthcare workers from the past as they check in on the dying? Or are the lights intended as warnings meant to keep the living away?

The poor souls that never made it off Rose Island were buried there. There are no grave markers, but at least two mass graves are known to exist in the island's wooded interior. In 1938, a water tower was built to ensure a freshwater supply to the lighthouse on the island. (The Rose Island Lighthouse went into service in 1870.) Workers constructing the water tower dug up a forgotten military cemetery.

The lighthouse keeper at the time, George Bell, reported they found scraps of uniforms, Civil War–era buttons, and human skeletons! But there was work to be done, so the remains and relics were stowed in a large metal box and reburied. Where? No one is sure.

Lighthouse keeping can be lonely, dangerous work, and many lighthouses are reported to be haunted. However, the Rose Island Light is not located in a desolate area. It is not some stark tower set atop cliffs being pummeled by an angry sea. No. The Rose Island Lighthouse looks like a nice family home that just so happens to have a big lamp on the roof.

You can go see for yourself, because today you can book a reservation and stay overnight. Want more ghost time? Stay the whole week and walk in the footsteps of Rose Island's former light keepers.

Charles Curtis became an official keeper of the light in 1887 and stuck with the job for thirty-one years, longer than any other Rose Island Lighthouse keeper. He would listen for the "sundown gun" to be fired from Fort Adams, the US Army base across the bay. When he heard it, he would lower the American flag and climb the tower steps to light the lantern for the evening. At midnight, he would climb the tower stairs again and make sure the lantern was still working properly. That is the time when guests staying at the lighthouse hear—and sometimes *see*—his ghost.

Maybe Curtis feels that these guests aren't up to the job of keeping the lighthouse, and

so he steps in to help. People who spend the night report that they were woken at midnight by footsteps coming down from the lantern tower and heading to the kitchen (Charles used to stop there every night for a glass of milk) before returning to the tower.

But it's not just footsteps that disturb guests at the Rose Island Lighthouse. Doors open and close with no one there. A figure wearing Curtis's usual baggy pants and suspenders has been seen walking through the keeper's house and along the lighthouse grounds. One guest even seems to have snapped a picture of him. This visitor took a photo of a glass-framed painting hanging in the lighthouse. When he developed it, a chill ran up his spine. There, reflected in the glass, standing just over his shoulder was the unmistakable mustached face of Charles Curtis!

Charles did not tend the lighthouse alone. He shared the island with his family, and it seems that his wife, Christina, might be one of the other documented ghosts. Their grandson Wanton spent much of his boyhood on the island. He came back years later to help with the lighthouse's restoration. Wanton's memories of "how things were" were vital to making the repairs accurate. While there, workers installed an antique kitchen wood stove. When Wanton entered the room, he immediately turned pale. He swore he saw the ghost of his grandmother tending to the stove. No one else saw the ghost, but everyone caught the sudden smell of freshly baked sugar cookies.

Now, that's the kind of ghost you might want to keep around!

Whether you visit Rose Island for one night or plan to spend the week, get ready for some eerie interactions. Whether it's with the friendly family of light keepers, the disease victims forced into quarantine, or the military members who are buried and reburied here, there will surely be stories you can share when . . . or if . . . you return to the mainland.

Stay a Night,
Stay a Lifetime

If you like ghosts but don't fancy a night in a haunted lighthouse, there are plenty of other places in Newport to stay. (But be warned— they are haunted as well.)

THE PILGRIM HOUSE INN

When the Revolutionary War began in 1776, the British saw Newport as the perfect place to house their navy. They could easily launch attacks on New York or Boston from the sheltered harbor. They took over Newport and occupied the city for the next three years. Newport would never be the same again.

The Pilgrim House Inn was built in 1775, just before the war. It is a three-story home tucked tightly in with its neighbors in what is now called the Historic Hill District. There are beautiful views of the harbor and the bay from the third-floor balcony. The British must have liked the "new construction," because this home and those around it survived the occupation while eight hundred other buildings did not.

In its almost-250-year history, the Pilgrim House Inn has had many owners and has been many things: single-family home, Navy housing, a homeless shelter for men, apartments for families, and now a bed-and-breakfast where guests come to enjoy the views, the garden, and Jessica.

Who is Jessica? At some point in time, a housekeeper at the inn felt the presence of a ghost who called herself Jessica. No one is really sure who Jessica was in life. It's possible she was the youngest child of the Currenses, a family of Irish immigrants who spoke of a baby girl in a letter that was never mailed to Ireland. Although, she could be the child of any number of families that lived in the house. In death, she is the spirit a young girl often seen wearing an old-fashioned gray dress.

There have been multiple sightings of Jessica on the long staircase leading up to the second floor. One particularly hot day, she was seen standing in the open front doorway, perhaps enjoying the cool breezes blowing up from the harbor. Some people have seen her looking out of a third-story window. Her favorite rooms to "play" in are Nos. 8 and 11— both on the third floor.

Jessica is a friendly spirit who enjoys tricks and fun and all things electrical and mechanical. She buzzes the intercoms in empty rooms and likes to start the dryer. When the house is quiet and everyone has gone to bed, she will play with a little music box. Guests have reported hearing not only the music, but also the sound of a child's laughter coming from rooms where no guest is staying.

Even with the many reports of Jessica's mischief, no one seems upset with her. How could you be angry with the spirit of a child who loved life so much, she decided not to leave?

THE NEWPORT ELKS LODGE

A little less than a half mile from the Pilgrim House Inn is another location with a spooky young guest. The Atlantic House Hotel was built on the corner of Pelham Street and Bellevue Avenue back in 1844. During the Civil War, the hotel was leased by the US Navy and became a temporary location for the US Naval Academy.

Well, you can imagine how busy an active Naval Academy would be. The Atlantic House Hotel certainly had its share of visitors, guests, and residents. It surely also had its share of hijinks and fun. The young men training here would soon ship out to war. This may have been their last home. This may have been the last place where they could relax and feel peace.

A few years after the Civil War ended, the Atlantic House Hotel burned down. A new building, the current Elks Lodge, was constructed in its place. Ghosts aren't just drawn to buildings; they are drawn to places. Although the hotel was gone, the land it stood on wasn't, and the new structure is just as vibrant and busy as the previous one.

Whether spirits have gathered here from the old Atlantic House Hotel or they have hung around from their days at the Elks Lodge, no one can really say. What they can say is that footsteps are heard around the lodge when there is no one seen walking by. The power spikes but there is no electrical cause. Lights will flicker off and on with witnesses seeing the actual light switches move!

The most notable spirit haunting the Elks Lodge is a young boy. He is often seen wandering on the second floor. Was he a visitor from long ago when the wartime Naval Academy was on these grounds? Was he a guest who stayed long after the hotel was gone? People believe he is the same boy seen with a woman in a portrait that hangs at the top of the stairs. It is said that when the child's image in the portrait is fuzzy or

blurred, the ghost is sure to be out and about. If you entered the Elks Lodge and climbed the long staircase to the second floor, would you be brave enough to examine the portrait? If the image of the little boy is blurry, would you hang around on the second floor and wait for his ghost? Or might you hurry back down the stairs and choose to visit the Elks Lodge on a "clearer" day?

THE PELEG SANFORD HOUSE

Peleg Sanford, one of Rhode Island's Colonial governors, built his home in Newport in the 1640s. The building didn't remain a home, however. It was enlarged and used as a business in 1827, and in 1845, it was enlarged again. The entire first floor was made a store with living quarters above. As odd as it may seem, the original house remains intact, just tucked inside this larger building. Today, the Peleg

Sanford House is still home to apartments and shops. The strange floorplan doesn't seem to bother the resident ghost.

Thomas, as he is known to the people who live there, is a quiet ghost. No footsteps, mutterings, or scary sounds from him. He is fond of animals and particularly fond of cats. And cats in the Peleg Sanford House seem to be particularly fond of Thomas. When Thomas is in the room, the resident cats behave quite strangely. Well, strange to the human eye. One cat weaves about as if rubbing herself on a pair of invisible legs. Another plays ambush and

launches herself out from under the furniture to attack invisible ankles.

Thomas has also been known to make his presence felt during parties and celebrations. It seems he especially likes to play with the electronics—turning things off and on. A guest at one celebration was headed toward the living room where everyone was gathered

when something caught her eye. There was the shadowy figure of a man in the kitchen. Was he helping himself to the food or pouring himself a drink? No. He was petting the family cat. The woman looked away for a moment, and when she looked back, he was gone. But the cat was still there.

Nobody is sure who Thomas was or why he chooses to stay at the Peleg Sanford House. But any spirit that stops to play with cats and likes a good party can't be all that bad.

White Horse Tavern

CHAPTER 5

Be Our Guest

Speaking of parties, Newport is known for its festive atmosphere! The city hosts the Newport Jazz Festival, the Newport Folk Festival, *and* the Newport Kite Festival. It was the original location for both the US Open golf and tennis tournaments, and the city is the location of the International Tennis Hall of Fame and the Hall of Fame Tennis Championships. Newport is also considered the "Sailing Capital of the World," and has been host to many America's Cup yacht races. It is the location of the National Sailing Hall of Fame.

When you invite so many people to come explore, enjoy, and play in your city, you want to make sure they have great food, great places to stay, and great entertainment. Sprinkle in a ghost or two and that's a good time for everyone!

THE WHITE HORSE TAVERN

The White Horse Tavern is the oldest tavern in the United States. However, it hasn't always been a bar and restaurant. Built in 1652, it was originally the home of Francis Brinley and his family. It didn't become a tavern until twenty years later, around 1673, when William Mayes bought it and converted it to a tavern. At the time, taverns were an important part of each town. They were a place where local residents met to eat and be with neighbors and where visitors could stop to rest and share news from places near and far. Taverns were so important to social life that some governments fined towns and cities if they didn't have one!

The British occupied the building during the Revolutionary War. The family that owned the tavern at the time moved away rather than have to serve the enemy. When the war was over, the family came back, and they went right back into business. If you visit the White Horse Tavern today, it looks very much like it did all those years ago. Don't believe it? Just ask the ghosts. They'll tell you it's true.

The most documented ghost is an older gentleman dressed in shabby colonial-style clothes who seems quite content to sit by the fireplace in one of the dining rooms. Occasionally, he does go upstairs to the men's room, where he has also been seen. It is believed he is the ghost of a guest who died in the tavern back in the 1720s.

He was a stranger in town, just passing through. When he was found dead in his room, his body was quickly removed and buried in the Common Burying Ground in an unmarked grave. Townspeople feared that the traveler had died from an infectious disease. Reports confirm that the owner's wife and a servant girl who had waited on him were sent to a quarantine island to make sure they hadn't caught anything and couldn't spread anything. History records that only the owner's wife returned from the island.

When a person dies unexpectedly and is not buried or mourned properly, they may choose to stay with the living. Could this unknown traveler from so long ago be the tavern's well-known ghost?

Another spirit takes on a more supervisory role. It is not known if the ghost is male or female, just that it tends to look after the building and keep an eye on the staff. Staff members have felt someone tap their shoulder and have also heard a voice tell them to lock up before the tavern's closing time. Some staff members report a definite presence when they are counting receipts or putting money in the safe.

There is a third spirit who first appeared in a photograph. A professional photographer was taking pictures to be used to promote the tavern. When

the pictures were developed, the face of a woman could be seen floating over one of the tables. Others have seen her walk around the restaurant before disappearing into the fireplace.

When a place is as old as the White Horse Tavern, with a long and interesting history, is it any wonder it will also have interesting ghosts?

THE HOTEL VIKING

The Hotel Viking may not be as old as the White Horse Tavern, but the ghosts there do know how to have a good time. It was built in 1926 for the purpose of being a five-star hotel for the rich and famous.

By the 1920s, Newport had become a summer playground for the very wealthiest Americans. Some families built themselves enormous and luxurious "summer cottages," where they held fabulous parties far away from the dirt and heat of the big cities.

For all of their grandeur and size, these summer homes strangely didn't have many bedrooms. It seems that the houses were built for partying, not for overnight guests. Where to stay then? The Hotel Viking!

The Hotel Viking has always known how to grant its guests' fondest wishes, and now those wishes can include ghostly tricks. There are reports of lights flickering on and off and cold spots being felt where there is no reason for a draft. There are reports of footsteps and voices being heard in empty hallways, and objects go missing from one place simply to be found in another. Think these ghostly happenings sound rather ordinary for such a ritzy hotel? Keep reading. After all, the hotel's guests were usually attending the best parties in the world. Maybe the guests didn't want those parties to end?

Before 2007, hotel staff reported hearing the sound of a loud party going on above one of the older ballrooms. Guests who had rooms in that part of the hotel would call down to the front desk and complain about the noises waking them up. Problem was, there was only a storage room located above that ballroom. Investigations proved that no one was in the space, let alone a party full of people. Still, reports persisted.

So, what happened in 2007? The hotel got a bit of a makeover—and the noises and complaints stopped. Had the phantom partygoers finally gone home?

It doesn't appear so. In 2010, reports of strange noises started back up again. But the noises no longer come from the storage area above the restored ballroom. (Hotel owners made sure to leave no empty space there.) Now staff reported noises coming from the lower levels of the hotel. Did the phantom party just relocate to a new space in the basement? At least the noise no longer seems to bother sleeping guests. But if you see a ghostly figure invite you down the stairs to where you hear the sounds of a loud and lively party, will you go?

THE CASINO THEATER AND THE FIREHOUSE THEATER

You may know that many actors and theater workers are superstitious and embrace the spirit world. For instance, when a show closes, it is appropriate to give the director a bouquet of flowers stolen from a graveyard. And one must always remember to put on the ghost light—a light that is left on at the center of the stage—before you leave for the night!

Theaters and ghosts have a long and active history, and the theaters and ghosts in Newport are no exception. Perhaps the energy and excitement of a live performance can't help but stir up the energy and excitement of the dead.

When he stepped onstage at the Casino Theater, a young actor forgot his lines. In his panic, he happened to look offstage into the wings. There was the figure of a woman trying desperately to get his attention. Once she had it, she whispered his line to him. He paused but for a moment before he and the play continued. When the show was over, the actor tried to find the woman so he could thank her for saving him. Not only could he not find her, but nobody else could find her either. No one had seen her, and there was no woman who fit her description backstage. Furthermore, the space where the actor swore he'd seen her was filled with sets and equipment. There was no way anyone could have gotten there. Had the man been rescued by a helpful fellow actor who just happened to be stuck there and knew his line? Or was she a theater ghost, looking out for the acting company and ensuring the play would go on?

In another incident, a group of actors was chatting during a break from rehearsal.

The subject came around to ghosts and superstitions, and one of the actors declared he did not believe in such things. Immediately, a stage light burst into smoke and flames. Before anyone could react, the smoke cleared, and the light worked like before. There were no burn marks or any other evidence of the event. Except perhaps that one actor had now changed his mind.

The Firehouse Theater has an interesting group of spirits. They don't seem to be from the acting community but rather from the time the building was a functioning firehouse. The cold-water faucet in the bathroom will turn on for no apparent reason. After the water runs for a bit, the faucet turns off as if the ghost has conducted a routine water flow check. As you can imagine, a strong and proper water flow is important to a firefighter.

The Jean Hunt House

It seems some theater-loving ghosts don't always stay in the theater. Sometimes they go home with the actors.

The Jean Hunt House was built around 1872, and for a long time, it served as a boardinghouse. Most of the people who lived there were actors, and the house—and the ghosts who lived there—had a lot of energy. Everyone (alive and dead) got along quite well. Residents reported hearing a young girl's

voice in the upper rooms, most often in the area outside of a boarded-up door. There were reports that an old man could be heard talking on the lower floors.

One actress reported that every night, as she went to sleep, she felt a gentle pressure on her chest. It was not uncomfortable or frightening but seemed more like a cat curling up with her for the night. The same woman reported that one morning, she overslept for a very important appointment. She was awakened when her blankets were thrown from her bed. She found them neatly laid out on her bedroom floor.

Sometime later, new owners bought the property. They wanted to turn the Jean Hunt House into their private family home. (And since it's now a private home, that's why it doesn't appear on the map key at the beginning of the book.) The actors were given notice to move out, which they agreed to do. The ghosts, on the other hand, didn't seem so happy about it. Loud banging started coming from the pipes on the first floor. And it continued until all the boarders had moved out. It was as if the ghosts wanted to scare off the new owners.

Once all the boarders had packed up and left, construction workers came in to renovate the house. Supplies and tools started falling from perfectly secure places. At one point, a hammer fell from a scaffold and severely injured a workman. Things got so bad, the construction crew refused to come back to the house. The owners called in a psychic to help, but when she arrived, she told the owners that

the spirit of "an old, angry man" was telling her to leave. So, she did.

Eventually, all strange goings-on stopped. The actors had all found new places to live. A new construction team came to finish the renovation, and it became a private family home. Did the ghosts leave with the actors? Did they finally make peace with the new owners? Or did the ghosts find a new place to live? No one is sure, but there have been no more mysterious happenings at the Jean Hunt House.

The Breakers Mansion

Mansions by the Sea

Built during the Gilded Age (1870–1900) by some of the richest people in the world, most of the famous Newport mansions were considered mere "summer cottages." Their owners only lived in them for six to eight weeks out of the year. Built to look like grand European castles, the main purpose of these mansions was to show that the owner had a lot of money and liked to spend it!

Much of the ghostly activity seen and felt around Newport's mansions takes place in the kitchens, the servants' quarters, or the stables. That is where people worked year-round, and that is where they may have accidentally died. Owners, on the other hand, only spent the summer there. They were not so deeply connected to their "cottage" that they wanted to stay after death. Except for one.

THE BREAKERS

The Breakers was built by railroad tycoon Cornelius Vanderbilt II. It was to be the summer home for his wife, Alice, and their seven children. Although the family had millions, they suffered personal tragedy after personal tragedy. Their first daughter, named Alice after her mother, died at the age of five from disease. Their second child and oldest son died from typhoid fever while away at school.

Soon after, Cornelius suffered a stroke and would not recover. Their next son, Alfred, went down with the RMS *Lusitania,* sunk by a German torpedo during World War I. He had bravely given his life vest to a woman who could not swim. And another son, Reginald, who lived a wild lifestyle, also died young. Alice Vanderbilt loved her family, but she had outlived most of her children and her husband. Her comforts came from spending time in her beloved summer home with her two remaining daughters and their families.

Soon after Alice died, so did her daughter Gertrude. It was Alice's youngest child, Gladys, who lived to a ripe old age and inherited The Breakers. In 1948, Gladys leased the property to the Preservation Society of Newport County for $1 a year with the understanding that the Vanderbilt family and their heirs be allowed to use the third floor of the mansion as it had always been intended.

Was this request made because the Vanderbilt children and grandchildren knew that Alice haunted The Breakers? It seems so, as the family reported seeing her apparition within a year of her death. Alice has been a constant presence at her summer cottage ever since. Many family members, tour guides, visitors, and staff have reported seeing Alice wandering through the mansion.

The family allows no investigators or ghost hunters to come and disturb her. Everyone knows who the ghost is, and she causes no mischief. Why should she? This is her beloved home.

BELCOURT CASTLE

It is not Belcourt Castle that is haunted, it is the items that were kept there. When many of the Newport mansions were built, they weren't just made to look like famous European houses. Some of them actually *were* European houses, or bits of them anyway: a fireplace taken from a French castle, stained glass from windows dating back to the German Renaissance, an enormous Russian crystal chandelier. These are just some of the treasures found inside Belcourt Castle. When you take historical objects from their home, sometimes the spirits that loved or owned them choose to go with them.

There is a monk who seems to have followed the wooden carving of a monk all the way from

Germany. He would wander around the castle close to wherever his statue had been placed—first in a family bedroom and then later near a first-floor bathroom. Now that the carving has been placed in the castle's chapel, the ghost monk seems much happier.

A ghost that looks like a samurai warrior is said to stomp around among the family's Asian art collection, and there are two medieval French chairs that don't like to be sat in. Reach for one, and you will feel a prickly sensation

in your palm. Sit in the other and you will feel energy pushing you out. One of the phantoms likes to borrow books from the library but always returns them. And there is an angry male voice in the French Ballroom that told one of the castle's tour guides to "Get out!" The guide felt uncomfortable for the entire summer tourist season and did not return the following year.

If you were told to get out by an angry disembodied voice, would you stay?

THE REEF
(LOCALLY KNOWN AS THE BELLS)

The Reef was the beautiful mansion of Theodore M. Davis—traveler, author, archeologist, and Egyptologist. From 1902 to 1913, Davis was responsible for the discovery of thirty Egyptian tombs, and his work would lead directly to the discovery of the tomb of King Tutankhamun—the famous Boy King.

If you study Egyptology, you will know that people believe artifacts left in a king's tomb are there for the king's use in the afterlife. If you remove them, you will be cursed. Either Davis didn't believe this superstition or he didn't care. Some people feel this is why The Reef suffered such a sad fate.

When Davis died in 1915, his collection of artifacts was given as a gift to the Metropolitan Museum of Art in New York City. It would be well looked after there. The Reef was not so lucky. It was sold to the Budlong family, who soon abandoned the house. During World War II, anti-aircraft guns were placed on the property, and the men who manned them were housed in The Reef. After the war, the home was once again abandoned. In 1961, it was set on fire by an arsonist. In 1963, what was left of the home was torn down. An unfortunate end to a beautiful house.

Was The Reef just a victim of unfortunate circumstances? Or was it the victim of King Tut's curse? We may never know.

Grave Accusations

Our Constitution makes sure the citizens of this country have certain rights. The right to free speech and the freedom of religion are in the First Amendment. That's what Rhode Islanders fought so hard for before agreeing to sign the Constitution. The Third Amendment says the military can't take over your house and live in it without your permission. (Bet the owners of the White Horse Tavern made sure that one was in there.)

There are twenty-seven amendments in our Constitution. That's a lot. But, for these ghostly tales, just think about the sixth one—which guarantees that you have the right to face and question anyone who accuses you of a crime.

REBECCA CORNELL

It was not uncommon for superstitions and dreams and visions to be used as "evidence" against people in Colonial times. Ever hear of the Salem Witch Trials? The Rebecca Cornell case doesn't involve witches, but it does involve a ghost—Rebecca's ghost—and it is possibly the most carefully documented murder trial of its time.

On February 8, 1672, seventy-three-year-old Rebecca Cornell sat in front of the fire in her bedroom. The night was cold, and she was tired.

Her son, Thomas, reported seeing her there before he went to bed. That was the last time he would see her alive.

In the morning, Rebecca was found alone in her room, burned to death. Perhaps an ember had sparked from the fireplace and caught her nightclothes? Perhaps after she'd fallen asleep, she slumped from her chair and tumbled into the fire? Whatever the cause, the coroner declared Rebecca's death an "Unhappy Accident of Fire." The family gave her a proper funeral and buried her in the family plot.

That would have been the end of it, and we may never have known there even was a person named Rebecca Cornell, except for what happened four days later. Rebecca's brother John Briggs was having trouble falling asleep. Just as he started to doze off, something violently tugged on his blankets! Standing beside his bed in a blazing light was the figure of a woman, burned about the face and neck. A very frightened John asked who she was.

"I am your sister Cornell," was the response. "See how I was burnt with fire. See how I was burnt with fire."

John decided this scary message meant his sister's death was no accident—she had been murdered. He swore out a statement, explaining what he had seen and heard. Rebecca's son Thomas was arrested and sent to trial.

Suddenly, everyone in town remembered stories of Thomas's cruelty toward and neglect of his mother. They swore Rebecca claimed he denied her proper food and refused to give her blankets on cold nights. Some said she'd mentioned committing suicide rather than have to live with her son for one more day. People said they heard these complaints, but no one ever saw Thomas abuse his mother. Besides, if all this was true, why had no one stepped in to help her before it was too late? Were these honest memories or were they fantasies?

Thomas doesn't seem to have been the most wonderful son—he was often in debt, and he and his family lived rent free in his mother's home. He did argue with her about chores and money, but would such squabbles really have led to him burning his own mother to death? The jury believed so, and Thomas was convicted. Over one thousand people came to see his execution.

Thomas didn't appeal his conviction. Why? Could it be because he was truly guilty? Or maybe he just felt guilty for how he had behaved. Whatever the reason, there was no solid evidence—except the testimony of a ghost who claimed she died from anything other than an "Unhappy Accident."

MERCY BROWN

Not all visions that appear in the night are considered ghosts. In 1892, the vision Edwin Brown saw was a vampire. It also happened to be his sister.

Look up "Vampire Capital of the United States," and don't be surprised when the answer comes back Rhode Island. Of twenty "confirmed" reports of vampire sightings, six lived in the "Ocean State." That includes the last known vampire: Mercy Brown. Now, Colonial New England vampires are not like the ones you see in movies. They did not suck blood from their victims' necks. Instead, people believed they drained your life force by sucking out your breath.

At the time, tuberculosis was responsible for the deaths of one in every seven people. It's a highly contagious disease of the lungs, and people who have it have a hard time breathing. They may cough up blood—or even drown

in it. (Yikes.) Not much was known about tuberculosis back then, especially not in rural parts of the country. Superstition and folklore held more sway over people's opinions than science and medicine.

Mercy was born into a rural farming family in 1873. Had she been born some seventy years later, she wouldn't be so famous and most of her family wouldn't have died so horribly. It is now known that the Brown family had tuberculosis. Mercy's mother was the first to die, followed by Mercy's older sister. Soon after, her brother Edwin fell ill. He was sent to Colorado in hopes the change of air and

climate would save him. It did. But before he could return home, Mercy contracted the disease. She died on January 18, 1892. She was nineteen years old.

When Edwin returned home, he became sick again. He became weak and pale. He had fevers and couldn't sleep. People started muttering about how the family must be targeted by the undead. And by undead, they meant a vampire.

One morning in March, Edwin came downstairs and told his father that Mercy had come to him in the night. He claimed she touched his chest and that he felt a terrible pain. When he woke coughing, he realized he was coughing up blood.

News got around, and the townspeople, quite terrified they would be next, demanded the bodies of the Brown family be dug up and examined. George Brown, the father of the family, objected to this, but scared and angry mobs are hard to stop.

When Mercy's mother and sister were dug up, they showed the proper amount of decay. When Mercy was dug up, she looked like she was merely sleeping. Her hair and nails seemed to have grown, and when a doctor pierced her heart, there was fresh blood. There was no doubt in the minds of the townspeople now. Mercy was a vampire. Her heart was removed and burned. The ashes were mixed with special herbs and water to make a potion—and Edwin drank it.

That is how you got rid of a vampire and cured its victim! But Edwin died in May.

Was Mercy Brown really a vampire? Why had her buried body stayed so well preserved? Well, Mercy Brown died in January. She was exhumed (dug up) in March. That's the dead of winter in New England. We know now that keeping a body cold also keeps it "fresh." When a body does begin to decay, the skin pulls back from the scalp and nails, making it seem like the person's hair and fingernails have grown longer. Mercy Brown was no vampire. And she was not responsible for the death of her family. In fact, her family—mother, sister, and brother (who she probably nursed while sick)—were responsible for hers.

A feverish and dying brother, suffering from grief and disease, dreamed he saw his sister. The rest became legend. Mercy Brown's grave is still visited by those who mourn her and wish her well.

The graves of Newport are many, and each name etched into the headstone has its own story. Even the mass graves of disease victims and the unmarked graves of pirates spookily reach out to make sure they are not forgotten. Rhode Islanders like to be heard; they like their stories told. Some of those stories are ordinary, but others are thrilling, and even others are quite fantastical. What kind of story will you leave behind? Or don't you plan on leaving?